Jessica Lundy

and

Your
Student Guide
to Success

D1069623

ISBN-13: 978-0-578-51776-6

Library of Congress Control Number: 2019905691

Cover Design and Back Cover Photo: The Monday Brand

Front Cover Photo: Q11 Photography

Published by Jessica Lundy International

Contents

Introduction

Success is something we all want to achieve but wouldn't it be nice to have a blueprint to acquire it much faster than expected? Succeeding is something that takes a lot of hard work, dedication, strategic planning, and wisdom, but there are short cuts that, if implemented correctly, can drastically change your circumstances seemly overnight.

As a child, my mother was always playing CDs of motivational speakers like Tony Robbins, Zig Ziglar, and many more in the car on the way to school. She was a huge advocate for personal development, and over the years, I became more interested. At ten, I created my first vision board and understood the power of confessions. I remember I was determined to go to Disney World. I had my mom order me the free Disney DVD that showed what your vacation could look like. I probably watched it over 100 times. I visualized my mother, brother, and I flying to Disney, staying in a hotel, meeting Disney characters, going on rides and bonding as a family. One year later my mom took us, and we had a phenomenal experience. At that point, I was too young to understand visualization, but I was thankful that it worked. What's even more exciting is that I taught my eight-year-old niece how to visualize and she went to both Disney World and a Disney Cruise in the same month.

As you're reading these stories, you might be thinking how far I can go with this? You can go as far as you like with the principles you will learn in this book. Your mind is the only limitation that can stop you from accomplishing your dreams. You'll hear me refer to mind shift throughout the book. This will be one of the primary keys to your success. It means to shift your mind from one way of thinking to another; from negative to positive, from poverty to wealth and from laziness to diligence. Remember, anything is possible if you can shift your way of thinking to believe it to be true. As you read this book, I want you to have an open mind and an open heart. It's not a coincidence that you are reading this book. Greatness is inside of you, and your destiny will be unlocked by not only reading this book but taking the time to do all the exercises and worksheets. They are necessary to stretch your way of thinking and creating instant action. Action is an essential key to success. There are a lot of smart people in the world that are unsuccessful because they didn't act on their goals, dreams, and most important, ideas. You were created to do something extraordinary in this world, and you must take action.

Chapter 1
Goal Setting Like a Boss

At five, I decided that I wanted to be on TV. I wasn't thinking Disney Channel or Nickelodeon; I wanted to be a talk show host. Every time I came home from school as a kid, my mom would be watching Oprah. And as I got older, it seemed like everyone was creating a talk show. From supermodel Tyra Banks to hip-hop artist turned actress Queen Latifah, and I wanted in on the action. Oprah Winfrey is a living legend. She's one of the top TV hosts of all time; the first black female billionaire, has a TV network, magazine and food products. She's just really crushing it. As a child, I was super inspired by her and wanted to create a similar empire.

When I was a senior in high school, all my friends were going to Miami and Cabo San Lucas, Mexico, for spring break vacation. I wanted to go, but my mother wouldn't agree to the unsupervised trip. But she agreed to take me anywhere else. After narrowing down my options, I convinced my mom to take me to Chicago to be on the Oprah Winfrey show. My mom had to write a few letters to Oprah's team because I was too young to be on the show. Meeting Oprah and her guest star comedian Chris Rock was an unforgettable experience that came out of perseverance and determination toward my goal.

Her talk show was epic but created for a more mature audience. My dream was to create a talk show specifically for young people. I would interview bands, talented entertainers, and young entrepreneurs. What I have learned about a dream is that sometimes you can set a goal, but if you do nothing to cultivate it, then it becomes a dream deferred. Having a vision and getting clear on what you want is just the beginning. And I didn't understand that when I was in school. In college I majored in communication. I knew I wanted to communicate in some capacity as my profession but didn't want to be a traditional news reporter/anchor. I went in a different direction and became an auto show product specialist and narrator. If you've ever been to an auto show and saw the people on the rotating platforms presenting the latest car knowledge, that was me. I loved traveling around the country with my friends, educating people on horsepower and torque, and all the details on the latest models. One day on the auto show floor, my life changed forever. I was narrating at the Las Vegas auto show and my friend runs up to me during my presentation and said, "Oh my God, I heard about this job that's perfect for you. You've got to apply for it." I replied, "I'm at work right now. And you're telling me about another opportunity. Maybe you should have texted me instead."

She was so excited for me. She didn't even know that my dream was to be on TV. What she knew was that I had a big, bubbly, larger than life personality and loved presenting to thousands of people. People have always told me I should be on TV. It's so important to pay attention when people continue to say positive things about you, or a skill set that you have. Sometimes you are too connected to your gifts and talents that you're unable to see how they can help you and others if you continue to cultivate them. As soon as I heard about this TV station looking for a host in my home state of Michigan, I made a decision that I had to win. The next day I flew back home to prepare for the audition. I got to the audition two hours early, and there were already 200 people in line. It's so important to show up to everything early including class, interviews, auditions and much more. Your first impression is your lasting impression, so please take my advice to heart and be early to everything. When I looked at the hundreds of people in front of me, I had to decide; I could either look at all the people in line in their professional attire and feel unworthy because they probably had more experience than I did and go home. Or I could say I am qualified. I deserve to be here just like everybody else. Being a TV host had been my dream since I was a child, so I built up my confidence and fought for my dream as I talked to the other contestants to pass the time. I recognized the person in front of me from a reality TV Show. To prepare for the interview, I watched every TV show and movie with anything to do with being a TV personality. From *Anchorman* to *The Newsroom*, I watched them all. The guy behind me flew in from LA and was already hosting national TV shows. Then I had to remind myself not to be distracted by everyone around me and all their accolades.

When you're working on a goal, it can seem like a world full of distractions are all around you. It's your job to take a couple of deep breathes and focus on yourself. What I love to do when I'm trying to focus on something, is put my ear buds in and tune out the world. My playlist included songs like *We are the Champions* and *Number One (#1)* by Nelly. You must do everything in your power to get yourself in the zone to accomplish your goal. It's essential to learn how to be your own biggest cheerleader because you might not have support from family and friends. At that moment, it was just me and my goal. And my goal didn't care about any of my excuses. It looked back at me and said are you going to fight for me or not? By the time my number was called to audition, I stepped up to the plate and gave it my all. Five auditions later, I got the job and was named the face of a TV network in Detroit. It was a phenomenal experience. From interviewing Usher and other celebrities to walking the red carpet, and being featured on national TV shows, it was such a huge life-altering opportunity.

The best way to win in life and win as a student is to set a goal. The key is setting a goal that is a bit of a stretch for you. It's all about getting to the next level in your academic performance.

Jessica Lundy

You're over 40% more likely to achieve your goals by writing them down, and the percentage increases when you share it with others as well. I don't want this to be the only time you ever write or share your goals. I want this to become a lifestyle habit of taking two minutes a day to rewrite your goals. I challenge you to tell your principal and counselors your goals and ask them if they have any resources or suggestions to help you accomplish them. For example, if you want to be a doctor, you can see if you can get an internship at a hospital. When I was in high school, I wanted to be an orthopedic surgeon and had a fantastic internship with one of the top surgeons in my state that wrote me a recommendation letter for college. You never know who your teachers, parents, and school administrators might know. It's always worth asking. I want you to become a professional goal setter and set new goals every semester. You've got this!

I am a Goal Crusher!

Goal Crusher Worksheet

What is your goal?

_____

_____

_____

What date/time will you accomplish it?

_____

What steps are you taking toward your goal?

_____

_____

_____

What daily actions are you committing to take?

1. _____

2. _____

3. _____

Who will hold you accountable for your goal?

_____

_____

_____

Have you asked for any help with your goal?

_____

What is your motivation to accomplish the goal?

_____

_____

_____

Date completed: _____

How did it feel to accomplish the goal?

_____

_____

_____

Chapter 2
The Power of Affirmations

After competing with over 1200 people to win my job as a TV host, I set another goal to be voted best TV host in Detroit. I had been on TV for less than one year. Some people knew who I was from winning the contest, but there were still many people that were unfamiliar with me, and I would need their support to win. Just out of curiosity, I looked to see who won the year before, and the winner had almost 20 years of experience. I remember going into my manager's office and being so excited. I said, "Oh my God, I'm going to win the best TV host in Detroit award." And he looked at me with a look of confusion like, how am I going to let her down and tell her she can't accomplish this goal. It was a little bit disappointing that my manager who had been one of my supporters since day one wasn't seeing my vision. I realized I needed to bring in more positive reinforcement. I already had clarity. I knew what goal I wanted to accomplish. But the next thing I needed was an affirmation. Affirmation is the action or process of affirming something into your life. It means to speak life in a specific area you need to see results. And that's what I did. I carried around a five by seven index card with my affirmation on one side and a mini vision board on the other side. I went to Barnes and Noble's to buy the magazine providing the award and wrote my name in as the winner. In my affirmation, I wrote that I would get thousands of votes and win the award. At the award ceremony, I would wear a red dress to match my TV station's colors and receive a standing ovation. I carried it with me all the time and would recite the affirmation several times a day. I said it so often that I believed it. I didn't look at my current circumstances. I only focused on my desire to win and the hard work I had done. I deserved this award. People will vote for me. I started putting together a full campaign like I was running for president. I had the posters, social media graphics, and was telling everybody to vote for me. Something indescribable happens when you speak the right things into existence. I not only got voted best TV host in Detroit, I received a beautiful plaque, got featured in a magazine, and got recognition at my job. My manager said that he was so proud of me for stepping out of my comfort zone and accomplishing my goal. And that's what life is about. It's about persevering. You might be working toward being captain of the cheerleading or basketball team or auditioning for the debate club, and somebody says you can't do it. You must tell them. Yes, I can, and I will. The best ways to prove somebody wrong is it to show them instead of telling them. There will be people that love you and care for you. But they might not understand your vision, purpose or gift. When they say things that aren't supportive, they're not trying to hurt you. They don't see the vision you see for yourself. And that's okay. You're the one that's responsible for you. You have to mentally fight for

your dreams. Repeat after me; *I Will Fight for My Dreams.*
I Will Fight for My Dreams. I Will Fight for My Dreams. If
you don't fight for your dreams, no one else will. During
school hours, you have amazing administrators, teachers,
and counselors that will help support you toward your
dreams and visions. They want you to win, succeed, and
have a full life. They genuinely want to help you, so utilize
the resources available to you at your school. Mentally
fighting for your dreams stops negative thoughts when they
come into your mind. Commit today to not entertaining
those negative thoughts because they will not help you
towards your goal. You've got to become laser-focused on
your goal so that you can accomplish it and have
unwavering faith. The more consistent you are with your
goal, the likelier it is to come to pass even faster than
expected.

When I was working on turning my dreams into reality,
I was saying I'm the best TV host every day while looking
at myself in the mirror. Some days I would ask myself am
I really going to win this award? I was so focused that
despite what my circumstance were telling me, I had to
win. And I made it happen. I've used the power of
affirmations in multiple areas of my life, including jobs,
interviews, tests, prizes, and gifts. I even won my
honeymoon by speaking it into existence with my fiancé in
the car on our way to a wedding expo. Every time I enter
anything, I expect to win because of the power of
confession. Randomly throughout the day, I will say, I Am
A Winner. I just keep saying it. My friends used to think I

was crazy until everywhere I went; I would win something. I'm the person that will walk in a store, and the manager will say, you're the 100th customer, here's a prize. I have these results because I declare out of my mouth, that I am a winner. So everywhere I go, I win. The same power is available to you if you have a mind shift. Believe that everyone wants you to win and succeed. Winning is a choice. Choose to be a winner.

I want you to understand today there is so much power in what you say which is both positive and negative. Generally, when people talk about affirmations, they keep it light, but I want to be honest with you and let you know the same power works to enhance or worsen your life. So, if you're a "Debbie Downer," then you're always focusing on negativity. You might say things like "no one loves me," "I always get bad grades," and "no one wants to hang out with me." All these feeling are false but appear to be real when you look at your situation from a negative perspective. Earlier I stated that winning is a choice; the same is true for negativity. You have to take a stand when negative thoughts come into your mind to not let them affect you and confess what you would like to see instead. For example, if a specific subject is challenging for you then it's your job to say, "I am great at math," "I get an A on all tests." The real key to positive confessions is belief. You can't just say the words; you have to believe it to be true despite how you feel or your circumstances.

Remember this with your social media post as well. If you're having a bad day, don't post about it. It brings everyone's energy down while their scrolling through their feed reading your post. Choose to be the person that's posting positive things, uplifting yourself and others at the same time so everyone can have a better day. I have a lot of people ask me if I'm happy all the time because I'm always smiling and in a great mood. The answer is no, I am human just like you, but as I stated earlier, I decided it wasn't fair to dump all my problems on my friends, family, and social media followers. If I don't like something in my life, I can either change it or choose to change the way it affected me. If you are in a severe situation, please let someone know, including your school counselors, teachers, and parents/guardians.

Now, I think you have a good understanding of affirmations and how to best utilize them in your life. The best way to learn a new principal is to put it into practice, and that's what I'm going to have you do now. The most effective way to change your mindset is to read these affirmations daily, so you start to believe these statements to be true for you. You can also create your own affirmations on the following page with specific goals you want to accomplish relating to academics, clubs/organization, future career ambitions, jobs/internships, and friendships.

Guidelines For Effectively Saying Your Daily Affirmations

1. Stand up while saying them
(Bonus: Looking at yourself in the mirror is best.)

2. Say them out loud with confidence

3. Say them with emotion/energy
(Bonus: Smile while saying them instantly makes you feel happy)

4. Listen to my *Wake Up and Win* with Jessica Lundy audio affirmation – Student Edition every morning to kick start your day

Jessica Lundy

Affirmations

I Am Setting Myself Up For Success.

My Teachers And Classmates Want Me To Win And Be
Successful Today.

Every Day My Self-Esteem And Self-Confidence Are
Increasing.

I Am Unstoppable, Resilient, Brave, And Bold.

Every Semester My Grades Are Improving.

I Will Graduate And Get Accepted To My Dream College.

I Am An Honor Roll Student.

Everyone Around Me Is Cheering Me On To Succeed.

Today I Will Take Another Step Toward My Goals.

I Am Ready For Today To Be The Best Day Of My Life.

I

am

Setting

Myself

Up

for

Success

Create Your Own Affirmations

I AM

_____

_____

I AM

_____

_____

I AM

_____

_____

I AM

_____

_____

TODAY I WILL

_____

_____

_____

EVERYDAY

_____

_____

_____

How does it feel to say your affirmations?

_____

_____

_____

What time(s) will you commit to saying your affirmations
(Recommended: Morning/Night)?

_____ A.M.

_____ P.M.

Chapter 3
Visualize Your Future

You've gotten clear on your goal, mastered affirmations, and now it's time to visualize your goal coming into fruition. Let's say you set a goal to be a doctor. Your affirmation would be I Am An Amazing Doctor, or I Will Go To Medical School, or I Am The Best Doctor In The World. After you say those declarations, the next layer to that would be to visualize it. There are two ways to do this best, and I recommend combining both methods. To visualize your future takes time and dedication. You can start by taking five to ten minutes in the morning and before you go to bed daily to create a movie in your mind of what you want to see come to pass. Let's go back to the doctor example. Take the time to see yourself graduating from medical school and helping patients. I love to turn on some very relaxing, soothing music, to quiet my mind so I can focus on the imagery of what I want to achieve. The coolest thing about visualization is it actually works. I have done it in so many areas of my life. I used to compete in beauty pageants in high school and college. Before I competed, I would close my eyes and visualize myself winning every competition. I also utilized it in school visualizing seeing an A-plus on the top my test. I used it in job interviews, I would close my eyes and visualize answering the questions to the manager, shaking their hand, hearing them say you got the job and calling my friends to share the news. The key to visualizations is similar to affirmations; it's all about emotions. I'm always in a state of gratitude and excitement about my goal coming true even before I see it happen in my life. My faith is so strong that my visualizations will become my reality, and they do time and time again. The first option will help you get in the right frame of mind to attract the things you want into your life.

The second option is to create a vision board. Creating a vision board can be a simple yet powerful exercise. You cut out pictures, phrases, and quotes from a magazine or online images and put them all on one board. They can be as big or as small as you like, it's entirely up to you. You can put all the things you desire on one board, or you can separate them by categories for your career, travel, college, and more. The purpose is to attract all the things you desire to have in your life. You can even get a group of your friends together or a club you're in and have your very own vision board party. I've spoken at a few, and it was an amazing experience. You can do this project inexpensively. Check with your school or library to see if they have old magazines they're not using and get some glue sticks/tape and poster board. You can also go to the library to print off pictures. The more specific you can be with your images, the better it will become. You can also ask your school counselors if they have any brochures for the colleges that you're interested in attending.

Wherever you want to go, you can get pictures of the campus or the logo and declare it in your life; I will get a full ride to this college or university. Once you're finished with your vision board, I highly recommend that you hang it up in a place visible to you daily and taking a photo of your vision board as well so you can have it with you at all times. When I'm really working on something, I will make my vision board my screensaver on my phone/laptop so I can visualize it happening throughout the day. I think that is a fantastic way to utilize these resources. From Olympians to entertainers, tons of famous people have used this source of inspiration.

Early in Beyoncé's career when she wanted to win an Academy Award, she printed out a picture of the trophy and put it right in front of her treadmill. Every day when she ran on it, she would look at the image and focus on winning. Beyoncé now has won over 300 awards including 23 Grammys and Guinness Book of World Records accomplishments. I would say those awards are worth visualizing a few minutes a day.

Notes:

Jessica Lundy

Everyday

I

Take

Sometime

To

Visualize

My

Future

Visualization

Action Step:

Now, I recommend taking a break from reading, playing the visualization music listed below and take some time to visualize the initial goal you set at the beginning of the book happening in great detail.

What did you see during your visualization?

_____

_____

_____

What action will you take as a result of what you saw?

_____

_____

_____

What time(s) do you commit to doing this daily?

_____

Bonus: I recommend adding an alarm on your phone with the time(s) you selected to stay consistent with this practice.

Here's a link to a free music track that you can download from Mozartt Music Group to enhance your visualization process.

Download Music: http://bit.ly/wuawvisualizationmusic

Create A Vision Board

Action Step:

Checklist

_____ Magazines

_____ Color Printer to Print Photos

_____ College Brochures

_____ Paper/Poster Board (whatever color you like)

_____ Glue/Tape

_____ Scissors

_____ Markers/Pens (You can write a title at the top/powerful words)

_____ Optional: Stickers and Stationary Accessories

Will you create it by yourself or with a group of friends/club or your family? (Who will you invite? If applicable)

_____

_____

_____

Jessica Lundy

What date/time do you commit to finishing your Vision
Board?

_____

Where will you hang it when you're done?

_____

_____

_____

On the next page, you have been provided a space to create
your vision board.

My Vision Board

My Visions Are Becoming My Reality

Chapter 4
Hold Me Accountable

I am so incredibly proud of how many actions you've taken so far toward your dreams. The next crucial step is accountability. The main reason that people don't accomplish their goals is because of a lack of accountability. Accountability means a willingness to accept responsibility for one's actions. Accountability helps you stay committed to doing your work. Earlier in the book, when I had you set your goal, you also set a date of completion as your first level of accountability to yourself. I'm a professional accountability partner; I keep my clients accountable on goals, whether it's starting a business or passing a state exam. I regularly help people with daily check-ins on the progress of their goal and what actions they've taken for the day. The feedback has been phenomenal. My clients have been getting more things done in a shorter time because they know they have to check in with me every day and I'll ask for progress.

Now it's your turn. I want you to take a minute and decide who would make the best accountability partner for you. You want to put some thought into this. Pick someone that you think is responsible, organized, and great with time management. If you have a friend who never turns their homework in on time, they might not be the best accountability partner for you. You also want to pick someone you don't mind talking to or texting daily to make sure you're staying on track. What's impressive is when someone sees keeping you accountable as a job how committed they become to help you with your progress.

I use my husband, mother, business coaches, and myself. But ultimately, where I'm at in my life, I mainly keep myself accountable daily. For some people family doesn't work because they might not enforce the consistency, but you can try different people on a trial base. Also, if you're in a school club or sport, that would be a great option to pick one of your fellow team members. You can check in with them before or after practice/meetings to keep each other accountable for your goals. Accountability might be a little bit out of your comfort zone, but that's okay because when you're trying to achieve success, you have to do things differently. This is your season to succeed at everything you do. If you've never had success before, it is now your time to receive it. Successful people keep themselves accountable. Having accountability partners has drastically changed my life and my business. My first accountability partner was my mentor in high school. He started as my tutor and eventually became my mentor. He regularly stayed on me to make sure I was remaining focused in school and passing my tests with 100%.

In the last couple of years, I have upgraded to being a part of mastermind groups. I have some fantastic mentors/coaches that are millionaires, and they highly recommend the power of masterminds. The most impactful thing they have taught me is that you can have anything you want; as long as you take action on it daily, and have someone keep you accountable on your goals. What I love about masterminds is the uniqueness of the members.

To create a mastermind group, you want to start by making a list of three to eight people you would love to meet with at least once a week for about an hour. While you're creating the list of people, you want to have in your group keep the personalities, passions, and unique skill sets in mind. You also want to decide who should be the primary facilitator of the group to make sure the meeting stays on time; so, everyone shares and remain on topic.

Also, just like with the accountability partner, you want to pick people that are responsible and can commit to making your scheduled time each week. Once you have your group, you'll want to agree upon a time, location, and topics you want to cover and rules that everyone should follow. The critical part of the group is to be consistent and have everyone contribute. It will stretch your intellect, create lasting relationships, and ultimately keep you accountable on your goals.

I am 100% Focused On My Dreams and Visions

Accountability Tracker

Goal you want to be held accountable on:

_____

_____

_____

Accountability Partner (name/phone number/e-mail):

_____

_____

_____

What day/time will you connect with them?

_____

How would you like them to keep you accountable?

_____

_____

_____

What daily action are you committing to?

_____

_____

How does it feel to have an accountability partner?

_____

_____

_____

What has worked for you?

_____

_____

_____

What needs improvement?

_____

_____

Mastermind Must Haves

Mastermind Members – Facilitator*

1. _____

2. _____

3. _____

4. _____

5. _____

6. _____

7. _____

8. _____

Date/time to meet: _____

Location (phone, Skype, in-person): _____

Topic of discussion: _____

Starter questions – What are you working on? What do you need help with on toward your goal?

How will everyone be kept accountable on their goal?

_____

_____

_____

Evaluate the group each month (What's working?)

_____

_____

_____

What needs improvement? Has anyone been absent multiple times? If so, what is the consequence?)

_____

_____

_____

Chapter 5
Network Your Way to Success

There's a popular quote that says, "Your network is your net worth." This is a crucial part of the goal-setting process. Jim Rohn states, "You are the average of the five people you spend the most time with." Strategic goal setting using this system might be a little out of the comfort zone for you and your closest friends and family. You have set a massive goal, wrote a specific affirmation for it, created a vision board, and have an accountability partner. Many people will stop after those steps, but I want you to stretch yourself a little farther to make sure you complete every goal you set now and in the future.

I want you to pause for a minute and think about your closest group of friends and their work ethic as a student. Are they striving for excellence every day? Are they clear on what college they want to go to and looking for scholarships? Are they early to class and stay after to ask their teachers questions if they don't understand something? Are they seeking a tutor if they need additional help in a particular area? Do they have a mentor, or are they a part of extracurricular activities? Or are your friends skipping class, bullying others and being involved in other disruptive behavior? If so, it is time to get a new set of friends.

Now, this is where the importance of networking comes in. To network means to exchange information and develop professional and social relationships. When I want to expand my network and relationships, I attend events and join groups with people I know I want to connect with. Recently, I decided that I wanted to take my business to the next level, and I joined a mastermind group with an elite association of people that have accomplished the goals that I have set for myself. The members in the group have not only held me accountable for my goals, but they have also become my friends, mentors, and people I can aspire to be like. When I look at my current circle of friends, I am inspired by each one of them, and they push me way out of my comfort zone to be the best version of myself. I want you to say the same about your closest friends.

Now it's your turn. Try to think of all the new places you can meet people. You can join a sports team or French club. Maybe try out for drama or student council. Some people meet while volunteering their time helping their community. You can always engage in conversation with more classmates before or after class. My daily confession is *Making Friends Is Easy*. I'm always smiling, happy, friendly, and helpful. These are some qualities that make you seem approachable to people at school and social gatherings.

Also, I want to bust a myth. When you're looking to make new friends, don't just try to be friends with the students that are popular. When you're filling out a scholarship or job application, they never ask you how popular you are or were in school. But they always want to know about your academic success, extracurricular activities, community involvement, and social skills. Being smart and hardworking is the new cool.

What that means is a lot of the smart kids that might have gotten teased because instead of going to the school dance or doing something fun, they were studying for a test or finishing a paper. These students should be celebrated for taking the steps necessary to succeed in every area of their life, which takes discipline. To succeed, you must be concerned with long-term gratification instead of short-term pleasure. A lot of those disciplined students are now the top people running tech companies, surgeons, lawyers, and are some of the highest paid people in the world. These are the people in school, focusing on accomplishing their goals and looking at the big picture. After reading this book and taking action with all the worksheets, I hope you become one of those determined, smart, big picture thinkers and doers that set yourself up on a pathway to success.

Earlier, I mentioned a quote that says, "Your network is your net worth." That means that your network (your friends) determines your net worth (how much you are worth financially). I don't believe anyone has a desire to be poor, but if you are hanging around people consistently making bad decisions, they are ultimately affecting your mindset, finances, and self-confidence. And so, what I like to tell students is that your GPA is usually a reflection of the Good People Around you.

Look at the people around you. Do you have good people around you that want you to get better grades, want you to be an honor roll student, are encouraging you to apply for internships and building you up to succeed? Or are they saying, why are you reading another book? Are they enhancing your life? Are they an asset? Or are they negative and a liability? If they are always complaining about their situation and not doing anything to change it, this is a red flag.

Later in this chapter, you'll be able to evaluate your friends and decide if the relationship is positive or negative. This exercise is something you should do alone so you can be honest with yourself. You have a straightforward question to answer, should I continue to be their friend? So, this is your wake-up call. You have only one life to live; live it as best as you can. This book has been all about taking action, so our last activity is all about networking and making new friends. If you're a part of student leadership at your school, then you've probably have attended a conference before and might be familiar with the importance of networking. When you go to conferences or summer academy, set a goal to meet different people. Remember, the purpose of networking is to get to know someone new, because they might become a friend, or you might work together in the future. So, I want you to set a goal to meet one new person a week every school year.

You can turn it into a game with your friends to see who can meet the most people. You can ask them their name and what they like to do for fun and establish a relationship with them. Building new relationships is something that you will always be thankful that you did. Working on your social skills is a critical skill set to acquire.

In school, I was in so many classes with people that I never talked to, and I wish I would have taken the time to get to know them better. I remember after I won the contest and became a TV host in my home state, I had a ton of people reach out to me that I didn't even know who went to my high school. We graduated together, and I regretted that I didn't take the time to get to know more people in my class and appreciate all the unique gifts they offer. The great news is you have plenty of time to do this. Repeat after me; *I Am A Networker!!*

Notes:

Jessica Lundy

My Friends Are My Biggest Supporters

Evaluate Your Relationships

Friends List (Name and add + for positive relationship and – for negative relationship)
Remember as you write out your friends list; ask yourself, is this person an asset or liability?

1._____

2._____

3._____

4._____

5._____

6._____

7._____

8._____

9._____

10._____

Based on your responses above, what is your next step with your relationships?

_____

_____

_____

How do you feel after going through this process?

_____

_____

_____

Networking Like a Boss

I commit to stepping out of my comfort zone and meeting new people each week.

_____(sign/date)

Where do the people you want to connect and be friends with hang out?

_____

_____

_____

What day, time, location and event do you plan to attend? (Remember this could be a club/organization/conference/social event)

_____

_____

_____

How did it feel to attend a new event/organization?

_____

_____

_____

Networking Comes Easily To Me

Conclusion

Congratulations, I am so incredibly proud of you. You have taken significant steps toward creating the life of your dreams. You have mastered goal setting, expanded your understanding of the power of words and how to use them most effectively throughout the day, practiced the art of turning your visualizations into reality, taken accountability to the next level and made new long-lasting relationships. I want you to take a moment to think about all the actions you have made completing this book. I've included some blank journaling pages in the back of the book as a space for reflecting on your journey.

The reason this book is called *Your Student Guide to Success* is because it's a great resource to guide you through your academic journey and beyond. I recommend rereading it and going through the worksheets at the beginning of each new semester to make sure that you're consistently setting goals with intention. One of the biggest things I have learned in life is every time I reread a book; I get new revelations in entirely different areas of my life. Now that I'm conscious of this, I look forward to reading the same book multiple times to find the hidden treasures I might have missed the first time or didn't need until I was in a particular situation.

I wish you so much success in your life, and I can't wait to hear about how you've utilized these principles. You can always send an email to Jessica@jessicamlundy.com with the Subject: Book Review/Testimonial or send me a message on social media @jessicalundytv on Facebook, Instagram, or Twitter and use the hashtag #wuawbook. Also, if this book has helped you please share it with a friend or let your teachers know about it too.

Notes:

Wake Up and Win

21 Day Goal Crusher Journal

Now that you are a goal setting rock star, I wanted to give you a bonus section to help keep you accountable for the next 21 days. It takes approximately 21 days to create a new habit, and I wanted to walk you through your first 21 days of the goal you set at the beginning of the book. All goals take a different amount of time to accomplish, but I thought it would help to give you a blueprint on how to achieve your goals.

Each day you will write out your main goal. Earlier in the book, I mentioned that you're over 40% more likely to accomplish your goal just by writing it down. Anytime I'm working on an important goal; I create a habit of writing it out daily, which has helped the goal come to pass even faster and strengthen my faith in accomplishing my goal with ease. I want you to commit to taking 10 minutes each day to close your eyes, relax, and visualize your goal becoming a reality. If you created a vision board, I want you to imagine everything you put on it happening in your life. You will also commit to taking daily actions on your goal and documenting the process. Being in an attitude of gratitude has not only brought joy and appreciation to my life but success as well. So, every day you'll list at least one thing that brings you gratitude. No matter what you're going through in life, there is always something to be thankful for; Whether it's breath in your lungs, clothes on your back, or the support of your family, friends, and teachers. Last, you will end with your daily confession. It is so important to speak positive words of affirmation over your life and to confess what you want to see.

Jessica Lundy

21

Day

Goal

Crusher

Journal

Day 1   Today's Date _____

Goal:

_____

_____

_____

Action Taken Toward Goal:

_____

_____

_____

I Am Grateful for

_____

_____

_____

Visualization (10 Minutes):   Yes   No

Checked in with Accountability Partner: Yes   No

Attended a New Event/Club/Activity: Yes   No

If so, where?

_____

_____

_____

Today's Affirmation:

I Am A Goal Crusher.

The best part of the day was

_____

_____

_____

Wake Up and Win

Day 2   Today's Date _____

Goal:

_____

_____

_____

Action Taken Toward Goal:

_____

_____

_____

I Am Grateful for

_____

_____

_____

Visualization (10 Minutes):   Yes   No

Checked in with Accountability Partner: Yes   No

Attended a New Event/Club/Activity: Yes   No

[63]

If so, where?

_____

_____

_____

Today's Affirmation:

I Start Every Day With An Attitude Of Gratitude.

The best part of the day was

_____

_____

_____

Day 3   Today's Date _____

Goal:

_____

_____

_____

Action Taken Toward Goal:

_____

_____

_____

I Am Grateful for

_____

_____

_____

Visualization (10 Minutes):   Yes   No

Checked in with Accountability Partner: Yes   No

Attended a New Event/Club/Activity: Yes   No

If so, where?

_____

_____

_____

Today's Affirmation:

Every Day, I Take Some Time To Visualize My Future.

The best part of the day was

_____

_____

_____

Wake Up and Win

Day 4   Today's Date _____

Goal:

_____

_____

_____

Action Taken Toward Goal:

_____

_____

_____

I Am Grateful for

_____

_____

_____

Visualization (10 Minutes):   Yes   No

Checked in with Accountability Partner: Yes   No

Attended a New Event/Club/Activity: Yes   No

[67]

If so, where?

_____

_____

_____

Today's Affirmation:

My Visions Are

Becoming a Reality.

The best part of the day was

_____

_____

_____

Day 5   Today's Date _____

Goal:

_____

_____

_____

Action Taken Toward Goal:

_____

_____

_____

I Am Grateful for

_____

_____

_____

Visualization (10 Minutes):   Yes   No

Checked in with Accountability Partner: Yes   No

Attended a New Event/Club/Activity: Yes   No

If so, where?

_____

_____

_____

Today's Affirmation:

I Am 100% Focused On My Dreams And Visions.

The best part of the day was

_____

_____

_____

Day 6   Today's Date _____

Goal:

_____

_____

_____

Action Taken Toward Goal:

_____

_____

_____

I Am Grateful for

_____

_____

_____

Visualization (10 Minutes):   Yes   No

Checked in with Accountability Partner: Yes   No

Attended a New Event/Club/Activity: Yes   No

If so, where?

_____

_____

_____

Today's Affirmation:

My Friends Are My Biggest Cheerleaders.

The best part of the day was

_____

_____

_____

Day 7   Today's Date _____

Goal:

_____

_____

_____

Action Taken Toward Goal:

_____

_____

_____

I Am Grateful for

_____

_____

_____

Visualization (10 Minutes):   Yes   No

Checked in with Accountability Partner: Yes   No

Attended a New Event/Club/Activity: Yes   No

If so, where?

_____

_____

_____

Today's Affirmation:

I am a Networker.

The best part of the day was

_____

_____

_____

Wake Up and Win

Day 8   Today's Date _____

Goal:

_____

_____

_____

Action Taken Toward Goal:

_____

_____

_____

I Am Grateful for

_____

_____

_____

Visualization (10 Minutes):   Yes   No

Checked in with Accountability Partner: Yes   No

Attended a New Event/Club/Activity: Yes   No

If so, where?

_____

_____

_____

Today's Affirmation:

Every Semester My Grades Are Improving.

The best part of the day was

_____

_____

_____

Day 9   Today's Date _____

Goal:

_____

_____

_____

Action Taken Toward Goal:

_____

_____

_____

I Am Grateful for

_____

_____

_____

Visualization (10 Minutes):   Yes   No

Checked in with Accountability Partner: Yes   No

Attended a New Event/Club/Activity: Yes   No

If so, where?

_____

_____

_____

Today's Affirmation:

I Am Setting Myself Up For Success.

The best part of the day was

_____

_____

_____

Day 10 Today's Date _____

Goal:

_____

_____

_____

Action Taken Toward Goal:

_____

_____

_____

I Am Grateful for

_____

_____

_____

Visualization (10 Minutes): Yes No

Checked in with Accountability Partner: Yes No

Attended a New Event/Club/Activity: Yes No

If so, where?

_____

_____

_____

Today's Affirmation:

My Teachers And Classmates Want Me To Win And Be Successful.

The best part of the day was

_____

_____

_____

Day 11   Today's Date _____

Goal:

_____

_____

_____

Action Taken Toward Goal:

_____

_____

_____

I Am Grateful for

_____

_____

_____

Visualization (10 Minutes):   Yes   No

Checked in with Accountability Partner: Yes   No

Attended a New Event/Club/Activity: Yes   No

If so, where?

_____

_____

_____

Today's Affirmation:

Everyday My Self-Esteem And Self-Confidence Are Increasing.

The best part of the day was

_____

_____

_____

Day 12   Today's Date _____

Goal:

_____

_____

_____

Action Taken Toward Goal:

_____

_____

_____

I Am Grateful for

_____

_____

_____

Visualization (10 Minutes):   Yes   No

Checked in with Accountability Partner: Yes   No

Attended a New Event/Club/Activity: Yes   No

If so, where?

_____

_____

_____

Today's Affirmation:

I Am Unstoppable, Resilient, Brave, And Bold.

The best part of the day was

_____

_____

_____

Day 13   Today's Date _____

Goal:

_____

_____

_____

Action Taken Toward Goal:

_____

_____

_____

I Am Grateful for

_____

_____

_____

Visualization (10 Minutes):   Yes   No

Checked in with Accountability Partner: Yes   No

Attended a New Event/Club/Activity: Yes   No

If so, where?

_____

_____

_____

Today's Affirmation:

I Will Graduate And Get Accepted To My Dream College.

The best part of the day was

_____

_____

_____

Day 14   Today's Date _____

Goal:

_____

_____

_____

Action Taken Toward Goal:

_____

_____

_____

I Am Grateful for

_____

_____

_____

Visualization (10 Minutes):   Yes   No

Checked in with Accountability Partner: Yes   No

Attended a New Event/Club/Activity: Yes   No

If so, where?

_____

_____

_____

Today's Affirmation:

I Am An Honor Roll Student.

The best part of the day was

_____

_____

_____

Day 15   Today's Date _____

Goal:

_____

_____

_____

Action Taken Toward Goal:

_____

_____

_____

I Am Grateful for

_____

_____

_____

Visualization (10 Minutes):   Yes   No

Checked in with Accountability Partner: Yes   No

Attended a New Event/Club/Activity: Yes   No

If so, where?

_____

_____

_____

Today's Affirmation:

Everyone Around Me Is Cheering Me On To Succeed.

The best part of the day was

_____

_____

_____

Wake Up and Win

Day 16 Today's Date _____

Goal:

_____

_____

_____

Action Taken Toward Goal:

_____

_____

_____

I Am Grateful for

_____

_____

_____

Visualization (10 Minutes): Yes No

Checked in with Accountability Partner: Yes No

Attended a New Event/Club/Activity: Yes No

If so, where?

_____

_____

_____

Today's Affirmation:

I Am Ready For Today To Be The Best Day Of My Life.

The best part of the day was

_____

_____

_____

Day 17   Today's Date _____

Goal:

_____

_____

_____

Action Taken Toward Goal:

_____

_____

_____

I Am Grateful for

_____

_____

_____

Visualization (10 Minutes):   Yes   No

Checked in with Accountability Partner: Yes   No

Attended a New Event/Club/Activity: Yes   No

If so, where?

_____

_____

_____

Today's Affirmation:

Today, I Will Take Another Step Toward My Goals.

The best part of the day was

_____

_____

_____

Day 18   Today's Date _____

Goal:

_____

_____

_____

Action Taken Toward Goal:

_____

_____

_____

I Am Grateful for

_____

_____

_____

Visualization (10 Minutes):   Yes   No

Checked in with Accountability Partner: Yes   No

Attended a New Event/Club/Activity: Yes   No

If so, where?

_____

_____

_____

Today's Affirmation:

Today, I Will Step Out Of My Comfort Zone.

The best part of the day was

_____

_____

_____

Day 19   Today's Date _____

Goal:

_____

_____

_____

Action Taken Toward Goal:

_____

_____

_____

I Am Grateful for

_____

_____

_____

Visualization (10 Minutes):   Yes   No

Checked in with Accountability Partner: Yes   No

Attended a New Event/Club/Activity: Yes   No

[97]

If so, where?

_____

_____

_____

Today's Affirmation:

I Am A Time Management Superstar.

The best part of the day was

_____

_____

_____

Day 20   Today's Date _____

Goal:

_____

_____

_____

Action Taken Toward Goal:

_____

_____

_____

I Am Grateful for

_____

_____

_____

Visualization (10 Minutes):   Yes   No

Checked in with Accountability Partner: Yes   No

Attended a New Event/Club/Activity: Yes   No

If so, where?

_____

_____

_____

Today's Affirmation:

I've Got This! I Can Do Anything I Put My Mind To.

The best part of the day was

_____

_____

_____

Wake Up and Win

Day 21   Today's Date _____

Goal:

_____

_____

_____

Action Taken Toward Goal:

_____

_____

_____

I Am Grateful for

_____

_____

_____

Visualization (10 Minutes):   Yes   No

Checked in with Accountability Partner: Yes   No

Attended a New Event/Club/Activity: Yes   No

[101]

If so, where?

_____

_____

_____

Today's Affirmation:

I Am Striving For

Excellence In

Everything I Do.

The best part of the day was

_____

_____

_____

Wake Up and Win

About the Author

Jessica Lundy is an award-winning TV host, media trainer, certified life coach and speaker, who is determined to help people live their best lives by adopting a winning mindset. From winning her dream job as a TV host in a major market after competing with over 1,200 people, to winning her honeymoon in beautiful Cancun, Mexico; Jessica embraces the power of attracting one's desires by having the right mindset and systems in place. Jessica is the creator of *Wake Up and Win School Tour*, an interactive workshop experience for students that educates, empowers and inspires them to achieve phenomenal success with her proven goal setting strategies.

To discover more about Jessica and her school tour or materials or invite Jessica to speak at your school or event, visit www.jessicamlundy.com. You can connect with Jessica on *Facebook/Instagram/Twitter/LinkedIn* @JessicaLundyTV. You can also contact her for bookings at schools or events by emailing booking@jessicamlundy.com.

WAKE UP AND WIN

Wake Up and Win with Jessica Lundy **Student Edition** is an audio affirmation album that will inspire students to have an incredible day. Listening to the audio everyday will lead to more focus in school, clarity, productivity, peace and happiness.

Jessica Lundy's
AUDIO AFFIRMATIONS

ORDER YOUR COPY TODAY!!!

www.jessicamlundy.com/shop

#wuawschooltour